The Missions of California

Mission San Fernando Rey de España

Jacqueline Ching

The Rosen Publishing Group's
PowerKids Press™
New York

For my father, Ching Tan

Published in 2000 by The Rosen Publishing Group, Inc.
29 East 21st Street, New York, NY 10010

First Edition

Book Design: Danielle Primiceri

Photo Credits and Photo Illustrations: pp. 1, 4, 10, 21, 22, 24, 25, 29, 30, 31, 32, 34, 45, 50 © Cristina Taccone; pp. 36, 38, 42 © Granger Collection; p. 27 © Varnel Jordan; pp. 28, 48, 49, 51 © Shirley Jordan; pp. 6, 14, 17, 33, 40 © Michael Ward; pp. 18, 43 © Tim Hall; p. 8 © Bridgeman Art Library; p.12 © Corbis/Bettmann; p. 14 © Superstock; p. 52, 57 © Christine Innamorato; p. 21 © Eda Rogers; p. 44 © Stock Montage.

Editorial Consultant Coordinator: Karen Fontanetta, M.A., Curator, Mission San Miguel Arcángel
Editorial Consultant: Thomas L. Davis, M.Div., M.A., California State University, Northridge
Historical Photo Consultants: Thomas L. Davis, M.Div., M.A. and Michael K. Ward, M.A.

Ching, Jacqueline.
    The mission of San Fernando, Rey de España / by Jacqueline Ching.
        p. cm. — (The missions of California)
    Includes index.
        Summary: Discusses the founding, building, operation, closing and restoration of the Spanish mission in San Fernando and its role in California history.
        ISBN 0-8239-5503-6 (lib bdg.)
        1. San Fernando, Rey de España (Mission: San Fernando, Calif.)—History Juvenile literature.
2. Spanish mission buildings—California—San Fernando Region—History Juvenile literature.
3. Franciscans—California—San Fernando Region—History Juvenile literature. 4. California—History—To 1846 Juvenile literature. 5. Indians of North America—Missions—California—San Fernando Region—History Juvenile literature. [1. San Fernando, Rey de España (Mission : San Fernando, Calif.)—History. 2. Missions—California. 3. Indians of North America—Missions—California. 4. California—History—To 1846.] I. Title. II. Series.

F869. S26C47   1999
979.4'93—dc21   99-21539
                                                                      CIP

Manufactured in the United States of America

Contents

The San Fernando Valley and Mission

Have you heard stories about the early days of California? Then perhaps you have heard stories of gold pouring from its rivers and streams. California gold was first found just north of the San Fernando Valley. However, years before the miners came to California, missionaries came from Spain. They built Mission San Fernando Rey de España in a place where miners would one day find gold.

The San Fernando Valley was home to many American Indian tribes. In fact, American Indians had been living in the Americas for thousands of years before the European explorers first arrived.

The San Fernando Valley inspired both the Spanish explorers and the American Indians to give it fancy names. Fray Juan Crespí, a Spanish friar, called it "Saint Catherine of Bologna's Valley of the Live Oaks." This name didn't stick. However, the names the American Indians gave to places in the San Fernando Valley are still in use today. Cahuenga Pass is a name that comes from the word *Kawengna*, which means "little hills." Topanga Canyon comes from the word that means "place where the mountains run out into the sea."

The mission built in this beautiful valley is called Mission San Fernando Rey de España. It was named after Saint Ferdinand, who was king of Spain over 500 years earlier. Rey de España means "King of Spain." Mission San Fernando was the 17th Spanish mission in the chain of 21 missions built along the coast of California in the 1700s and 1800s.

Mission San Fernando was founded in 1797 by Fray Fermin Francisco de Lasuén. The community at the mission began with a few Spanish missionaries and soldiers and members of the Chumash and

The welcoming entrance to Mission San Fernando Rey de España.

▲

*Amerian Indians welcome travelers to stay at Mission
San Fernando Rey de España.*

Tongva Indian tribes from the region. Two months after the mission was founded, the community included over 40 American Indians. By 1822, over one thousand Indians lived as a part of the mission community.

Unlike many of the other missions, which were built in the wilderness, Mission San Fernando was built close to the growing *pueblo* of Los Angeles. *Pueblo* is the Spanish word for a village or settlement that is unrelated to the missions. Today, Los Angeles is such a large city that

 6

it is hard to imagine that it was once a small farming community.

The San Fernando mission community produced many things, such as candles, soap, and wine. The American Indians who lived and worked at the mission were very skilled at making leather goods. They made shoes, clothes, saddles, and rawhide strips (used for building) out of leather. They were also known for their skill at ironwork. They made hinges, scissors, cattle brands, plows, and other tools. All these things could be sold to people in the nearby *pueblo* of Los Angeles.

Mission San Fernando also became known to travelers on El Camino Real. This was the main road that went up and down Alta California (what is today known as California), linking the missions together. Travelers were welcome to stay for free at the mission, and they usually left spreading word of the delicious wines they had tasted there. In turn, the travelers reported the latest news to the missionaries.

Spanish Settlement of Alta California

Over two centuries before Mission San Fernando was built, Europeans began exploring the Americas. Colonists from England, France, and the Netherlands built settlements there. However, it was Spain that settled the largest area of land. By 1536, Spain's overseas empire, called New Spain, included present-day Mexico, the Antilles, the Philippines, Central America, half of South America, and much of the United States.

Yet, before 1769, no settlements had been built in Alta California. Up until then, very little was known about this large territory. No settlers had shown any interest in going there. There were no land routes and it would not have been easy to get food, clothing, and other supplies.

Then King Carlos III of Spain heard that the Russians were interested in settling the land. Since 1740, the Russians had explored Alaska and built settlements there. They began to move farther and farther south. King Carlos III knew that Alta California was too important for Spain to lose to the Russians. The land was important because it was rich, fertile, and near the sea. It was a perfect place to build towns and harbors for ships.

The Spanish government decided that a chain of missions would be set up along the coast of Alta California. Spanish friars would settle there, with soldiers at presidios, or military forts, nearby. It was the soldiers' job to protect the missions.

The Rise of the Missions

From 1769 to 1823, the Spaniards built 21 missions along the coast of Alta California. Since the 1400s, Spain had found that

8

King Carlos III decided that establishing missions would be a good way to settle land. ▶

▲

Fray Junípero Serra is known as the father of the missions.

missions were a good way to begin settling a territory. Spanish missionaries were sent around the world to convert people to Christianity (to follow the teachings of the Bible and Jesus Christ).

The man who led the first group of missionaries to Alta California was Fray·Junípero Serra. He was born in Majorca, Spain, and joined the Franciscan order at the age of 16. Before becoming a missionary, he was a university professor and a preacher. He became the first president of the California missions and is known as the father of the missions. In his lifetime, Fray Serra founded 9 of the 21 California missions.

Some students of the California mission period have claimed that Fray Serra was cruel to the American Indians. Others view him as a man who truly cared for the Indians. They point out that the documents from the missions do not show that Fray Serra ever mistreated the Indians. There is no question, however, that Fray Serra was devoted to the Christian faith and to spreading its message.

The Purpose of the Missions

From the Catholic Church's point of view, the main goal of the missions was to convert the local American Indians to Christianity and turn them into productive tax-paying Spanish citizens. American Indians were recruited to the missions and the newly converted were called neophytes. The Spanish king and church leaders believed it was their Christian duty to convert the American Indians and to make them "civilized," as well as to protect them. The Spanish believed the Indians could only become "civilized" by learning to live and work in the European way.

Many American Indians were baptized and converted. A baptism was the Christian ritual the friars performed to

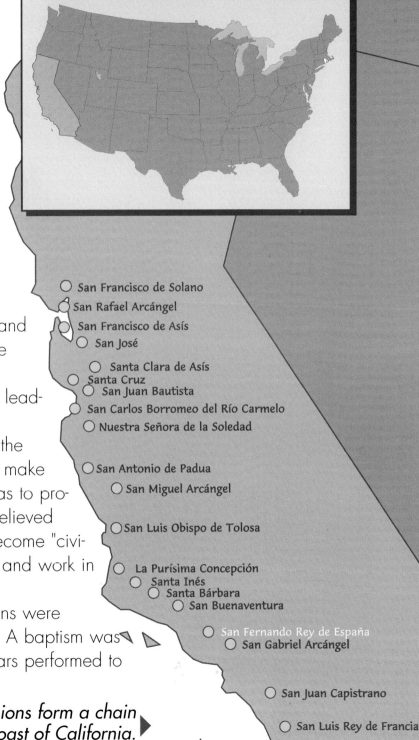

- ○ San Francisco de Solano
- ○ San Rafael Arcángel
- ○ San Francisco de Asís
- ○ San José
- ○ Santa Clara de Asís
- ○ Santa Cruz
- ○ San Juan Bautista
- ○ San Carlos Borromeo del Río Carmelo
- ○ Nuestra Señora de la Soledad
- ○ San Antonio de Padua
- ○ San Miguel Arcángel
- ○ San Luis Obispo de Tolosa
- ○ La Purísima Concepción
- ○ Santa Inés
- ○ Santa Bárbara
- ○ San Buenaventura
- ○ San Fernando Rey de España
- ○ San Gabriel Arcángel
- ○ San Juan Capistrano
- ○ San Luis Rey de Francia
- ○ San Diego de Alcalá

The 21 missions form a chain along the coast of California. ▶

convert the American Indians to Christianity. The friars believed that they were saving the souls of the Indians by making them part of the Catholic Church. Once they were converted, the Indians took part in other Catholic rituals.

The missionaries attracted the American Indians to the mission by giving them beads, blankets, cloth, ribbons, and food as gifts. Once converted, the American Indians were supposed to do Christian work by building mission structures and raising crops and livestock. Some American Indians tried to teach the outsiders their way of life, but most Europeans believed they had nothing

When the Indians were baptized, they were considered citizens of Spain.

to learn from the Indians.

Although mission life offered the Indians shelter, a steady food supply, and the opportunity to learn new skills, it deprived them in some ways, too. In order to become part of the religious community of the missions, Indians had to give up their cultural, religious, and even physical freedom.

The California missions were built about a day's ride apart from each other on the best farming lands. The Spanish missionaries did not see the land as their own. They believed that once the American Indians had learned the Christian way of life and worship, and took on the responsibilities of being a Spanish citizen, the land could be returned to them. The Spanish thought this would take no more than 10 years, but it didn't turn out that way. The Indians ended up losing most of their land and much of their culture.

For the American Indians, life was different from mission to mission. There were incidents of cruel treatment, especially at the hands of the soldiers. Some of the American Indians tried to escape and if they were already baptized, the soldiers went looking for them. Other Indians stayed at the missions because they saw it as the only way to survive. Still others lived full lives at the missions and felt true affection for the Spanish friars.

13

Before the Spanish: The American Indians

The Spanish Meet the Chumash Indians

Some American Indian tribes welcomed the outsiders and others did not. One reason that the missionaries chose the San Fernando Valley for its 17th mission is that the American Indians of the area were friendly.

In 1769, a missionary explorer named Fray Juan Crespí met some of the Chumash Indians who lived in the San Fernando Valley. Fray Crespí had been a student of Fray Serra's and was known for recording details of his expeditions with other missionaries. While exploring the San Fernando Valley area in search of a way north to find Monterey Bay, he and a small group of friars and soldiers stopped to make camp. Fray Crespí wrote in his diary that many local Indians came to visit the camp. Each Indian brought food as a gift to the Spaniards, and in return, the Spaniards gave them beads and ribbons.

Many of the tribes in the San Fernando Valley shared the same culture and spoke different dialects of the same language. When the Spaniards came, they identified all of these tribes as either Fernandenos or Gabrielinos. They were named after Missions San Fernando and San Gabriel. About 4,000 Fernandenos and Gabrielinos lived in the area at the time Mission San Fernando was built.

Today, the descendants of tribes from this area do not call themselves by these Spanish names. Instead, they use American Indian names. The main tribes represented at Mission San Fernando were the Chumash and the Tongva.

The Chumash Indians lived to the north of the Tongva Indians, mostly in the area that is now Ventura County. Both tribes also lived on the

◄ *The Chumash Indians drew pictographs, or paintings, on the walls of caves.*

The Chumash Indians built 30-foot canoes called tomols.

Santa Barbara Channel Islands off the Alta California coast. There were five or six times as many Chumash Indians as there were Tongva Indians. They were the largest group of American Indians living in Alta California when the Spanish settlers arrived.

The Spanish thought the Chumash were the most advanced of all the American Indian tribes. The Chumash were skilled craftsmen who could weave beautiful blankets out of feathers, make amazing baskets, and

16

build 30-foot canoes called *tomols*. The Chumash had also developed a system of astronomy.

Ancient Peoples: Their Way of Life

American Indians had lived on the land along the Pacific Ocean for thousands of years before the Europeans came. The Tongva descended from the Shoeshone people who came from the Great Basin and Mojave Desert, farther inland. When the Tongva arrived in coastal Alta California, the Chumash Indians were already living there.

The Chumash and Tongva Indians had many things in common. Tribes were lead by a council of elders. Elders passed down traditions from generation to generation. Music and dance were important to every part of their daily life. They sang songs for harvesting, hunting, warfare, and births. They played musical instruments, such as rattles made from turtle shells and whistles made from wood.

The large houses of the Chumash and Tongva were shaped like domes. The frames of the houses were made of poles. Sometimes these poles were made from sycamore or willow trees. Other times they were made from whale ribs. Over this frame hung a thatch roof built from wild alfalfa, fern, tree bark, and

▲

The domed-shaped houses of the Chumash Indians were large enough to house several families.

▲

Fishing was an important source of food for the Chumash Indians.

other plants.

Several Indian families could live in one of these houses. In addition to building large settlements, these Indians also built small camps farther away where one or two families might live for a week or even a season. The camps were built as temporary shelters. As hunters and gatherers, the Indians moved around with the changing seasons.

The Chumash and Tongva mainly ate wild plants and seeds, and if the hunting was good, they had deer or rabbit. Fish was an important food for the tribes who lived on the coast. There were also other marine animals to be caught, such as ducks, clams, and mussels. To catch fish, the Chumash made hooks from animal bones and tar. The Tongva twisted cactus thorns into the shape of hooks.

Both tribes drew pictographs, or paintings, on the walls of caves. In this way, they told the stories of their way of life. They made the colors from different rocks and minerals. The Tongva used red, white, and black. The Chumash Indians used up to six different colors.

Some Indian tribes, such as the Chumash, buried their dead, but the Tongva cremated theirs. The body of the deceased was burned in a pit. The Chumash who lived in the area of the San Fernando Valley kept cemeteries. They marked their graves with baskets, whale bones, or stone.

Many things can be learned from these American Indian graves, such as how people used to live. In May 1997, a Chumash grave was found with clay bowls, whistles, and smoking pipes nearby. Many people are interested in the discovery, preservation, and study of historical artifacts, or things made by people. Many American Indians consider these graves to be sacred or holy. It is important to remember the connection these gravesites have to the American Indians living today.

Founding Mission San Fernando

Fray Fermin Francisco de Lasuén

When Fray Junípero Serra died in 1784, Fray Lasuén was the friar who took over for him. He took charge of bridging the distance between Missions San Gabriel and San Buenaventura by founding a new mission between them. This was Mission San Fernando Rey de España, which was 25 miles north of the *pueblo* of Los Angeles.

Fray Lasuén joined the Franciscan order when he was 23 years old. Soon after his training, he was sent away from his homeland of Spain to be a missionary in Mexico. In 1767, he became an assistant to Fray Serra.

Fray Lasuén was the right man to take over Fray Serra's work. He was a hard worker, founding a total of nine missions. In 1797, his busiest year, he founded four of the missions! He was 61 years old that year. He also oversaw the rebuilding of original mission buildings. Under his guidance, the missions grew and became successful. Many American Indians were converted to Christianity. The period when Fray Lasuén was mission president is known as the Golden Age of the Missions.

The Beginnings of Mission San Fernando

The spot that Fray Lasuén picked for the 17th mission was on land that had been granted to Francisco Reyes, mayor of the Los Angeles *pueblo*. Reyes fought to keep the land, but was forced to give it up to the missionaries. Later, he became godfather to the first child baptized at the mission.

Fray Lasuén had great hopes for the future of the American Indians. ▶

The living quarters for the first bishop of California at Mission San Fernando.

On September 8, 1797, Fray Lasuén opened the new Mission San Fernando Rey de España in honor of Saint Ferdinand. A few missionaries and neophytes had come from Missions Santa Bárbara and San Buenaventura to celebrate the new mission. A *ramada*, or shelter of branches, was built to shelter the celebrants. The Indian musicians

 22

brought their instruments to perform the Christian songs and chants they had learned. On that day, 10 American Indian children were baptized.

Fray Francisco Dumetz from Mission San Buenaventura and Fray Juan Cortés from Mission San Gabriel came to take charge of the new mission at San Fernando. Their first task was to begin work on the buildings that would make up the mission. A few weeks after the opening of Mission San Fernando, there were crude living quarters for the guards and missionaries, a temporary church, and a storeroom. In keeping with custom, the nearby missions sent livestock and seeds to help the new mission get started.

Less than a year after the founding of Mission San Fernando, Fray Cortés left. The mission came under the care of many different friars after that. In 1820, Fray Francisco Ibarra was put in charge. He was a strong-willed man who worked hard to keep the mission a success. Unfortunately, he could not overcome the problems that would later plague all of the California missions.

Building the Mission

Mission San Fernando was one of the largest missions in Alta California. There were so many neophytes that they had to keep expanding the buildings. It was said that if all the buildings were lined up, they would measure a mile.

By November 1797, the small chapel was built with adobe, sun-dried bricks made of straw, mud, and manure. Adobe was used by the Spanish in Spain and Mexico because it kept cool in the summer and warm in the winter. Naturally, it was also a good building material for the missions. Around the same time, a granary, a weaving room, and a storeroom were added.

The mission community grew very quickly. By 1799, the chapel was too small to fit the growing number of neophytes and had to be rebuilt. Other mission buildings, including the friars' living quarters, had to be enlarged. The neophytes, under the direction of the friars, continued to expand or repair the buildings as needed in the years to come.

Separate houses to the east and west of the mission were built for neophyte families, forming a village. As the number of neophytes grew over the years, little adobe houses were added to this village.

Traditionally, missions were designed as a quadrangle, a four-sided enclosure around which the mission buildings stood. In 1802, a building was raised to complete the quadrangle of Mission

Many missions were built with adobe or sun-dried bricks.

The fountain at Mission San Fernando Rey de España.

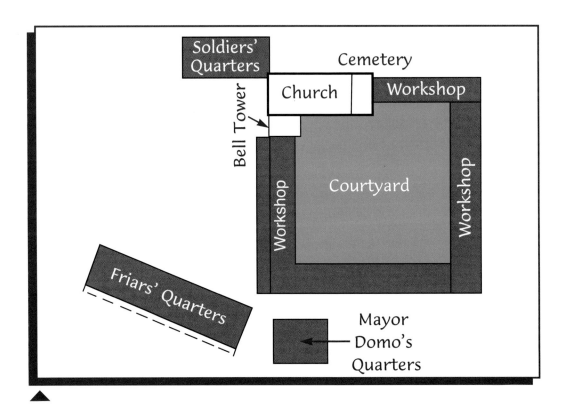

This is the basic layout of Mission San Fernando.

San Fernando. It was made up of a storeroom, a carpenter shop, and granaries.

In 1806, a large, permanent church was completed. The church measured 185 feet by 35 feet. The church walls appear to lean outward, as they were built five feet thick at the base and only three feet thick at the top. On one side of the chapel, a staircase led up to the two-story bell tower. Three arched openings held the mission's three bells. A large fountain and basin were built in the courtyard. The neophytes used their artistic talents to paint the mission walls. Images of flowers, vines, seashells, and animals decorated these walls.

In most of the missions, the church was connected to the *convento*, or the friars' living quarters. However, the present-day *convento* at Mission San Fernando was a later addition, so it was built apart from the quadrangle. A beautiful corridor, with 21 Roman arches, connected the *convento* to the church.

So many visitors traveling on El Camino Real came to Mission San Fernando that the friars decided to add more guest rooms to the *convento*. More and more rooms were added over a period of 12 years, until the *convento* became the largest building of all the missions. It became known as the "long building." When this two-story building was completed in 1822, it contained over 20 rooms, a reception room, kitchen, storehouse, winery, refectory (dining hall), and chapel.

Mission San Fernando had a reputation for its excellent wines. Around the structure of the mission walls, the mission community, aided by the warm climate, grew over 30,000 grape vines and 70 acres of olive trees. The neophytes collected the olives and crushed them to make olive oil.

In December of 1812, an earthquake shook the mission and damaged these buildings. Afterward, 30 new beams were added to strengthen the walls. The new beams helped the buildings to withstand other earthquakes.

▲

A fountain in the mission courtyard.

27

Daily Life at the Mission

The schedule of daily life was set by the ringing of bells.

The Typical Workday

At Mission San Fernando, the chapel bells played an important role in daily life. The bells rang in the morning to wake up the neophytes. They rang at different times throughout the day to call them to breakfast, church, lunch, and chores. Neophytes who did not obey these calls or do the work expected of them were punished.

At dawn, everyone, except the sick, went to Mass, the main religious ceremony. Sometimes, a neophyte who had been taught by the friars would lead the prayers. The prayers were recited in the local language, as well as in Spanish.

After Mass, everyone ate breakfast. Small children ate with their parents at home in the village. The older boys ate at the community kitchen, and the girls 13 years and older ate in the *monjerío*, the living quarters for unmarried girls. Everyone drank hot chocolate and ate *atole*, porridge made from cooked corn. *Atole* would be served again at lunch and dinner along with fruit, vegetables, and chicken or beef.

Around 8:00 A.M., everyone over the age of nine began morning chores in the fields or in the shops. Children under the age of nine went to church for religious classes. The friars also taught the children to sing

A side view of the mission archives building. ▶

hymns. The American Indians loved to sing.

Between 11:00 A.M. and 2:00 P.M., a midday meal was eaten. The *atole* might be served with mutton (a meat made from sheep) or beans. There were also tortillas, flat cakes made of ground meal.

Work stopped for *siesta,* the afternoon rest or nap, and began again around 4:00 P.M. The men spent the rest of the day working in the fields or on the buildings. They herded the cattle, horses, and sheep. They grew wheat, barley, peas, beans, corn, figs, and peaches. When harvest season ended, they made adobe bricks from soil

A small kitchen at the mission.

Small children ate with their parents at home in the village.

mixed with water and straw or made tiles from clay.

Out in the vineyards and in the wine factory, the neophytes produced the wine that Mission San Fernando became famous for. To make the wine, the Indians washed their feet in a basin before stepping into the large vats filled with ripe grapes. Then they pressed the grapes by stamping down on them. The juice drained into wooden pipes that

This wall menu lists the food cooked at the mission.

led into barrels in a wine cellar. It would stay there until it turned into wine. At the peak of its wine production, Mission San Fernando produced 2,000 gallons of wine and 2,000 gallons of brandy each year.

The women weaved in workrooms, producing much of the cloth used at the mission, including blankets, sheets, tablecloths, towels, and napkins.

Free Time at the Mission

At 5:00 P.M., the bells rang to signal the end of the workday and to call everyone back to church to pray. This was followed by supper, after which there was time for games, gambling, and other pastimes.

One of the games the Chumash Indians played, called *shinny*, was like an early kind of hockey. It was played on a large open field with two teams. Each team used sticks to shoot a small wooden ball through the other team's goal post. The team with the most goals won.

The Tongva Indians played a game called *wauri*. One player would put eight playing pieces under a basket. The pieces were made of reed (a tall grass) and colored on one side. Another player would guess the number of pieces facing up. Many of the Tongva and Chumash games involved gambling by the players and spectators. These games could continue until 8:00 P.M., when everyone at the mission went to sleep.

Saturdays were sometimes workdays, but on Sundays and holidays, everyone was allowed to rest and play after a few hours of prayer. The Catholic Church had many patron saints and for each patron saint, there was a holiday, which they called a holy day.

A Different World

The neophytes were taught only what the missionaries thought was needed to make them good Christians and good productive citizens of Spain. The friars taught them to read and write in both Spanish and

▲

The Chumash Indians played shinny, a type of hockey.

▲

Gathering food was an important means of survival for the Indians.

Latin, so that they could understand the Bible. In turn, the neophytes taught the friars their languages. When the friars heard confession, a Catholic ritual in which a person tells his or her sins, it was in the neophyte's own language.

The Chumash and Tongva Indians taught their children tribal customs, proper behavior, and the skills they needed to survive. They taught them by telling stories or by setting an example. They did not have schools like the European children had.

The neophytes lived a life of order at the missions, but it was a life very different from the one they had known. For thousands of years, American Indians had hunted and gathered food to survive, so they knew how to work hard. Usually, they worked extremely hard for a brief period of time and then rested. At the mission, however, they had to work long hours without rest.

It was hard for the American Indians to understand the need to work all day, every day. Why should anyone work like this if there was no danger of running short of food?

The friars believed that they were helping the neophytes by teaching them the value of hard work. However, some American Indians did not like working in this manner. They wanted to roam the earth, hunt, eat what they wanted to, wake up when they wanted to, play games and work as they saw fit. If and when their desire for freedom became too strong, they would run away. Most American Indians, when asked why they had run away from their mission, said they had felt like they were in jail.

There were always some American Indians trying to escape from the mission. The neophytes' attempts at escaping were usually unsuccessful. The soldiers were sent out to capture baptized runaways, and punishment, if the neophytes were caught, was harsh.

The friars continued to believe that they were saving the souls of the American Indians. They saw the neophytes as adult children who had to be taught the right way to behave. Turning the Indians into good Christians and good citizens was considered the only important thing.

Today, we realize the importance of having respect for diverse cultures. We understand that one culture is not superior to another culture just because it is different. The mission system brought new skills to the California Indians, but in some ways it deprived them of their own culture and freedom.

Troubled Times

Toward the end of his life, Fray Lasuén stopped founding missions. Instead, he had to maintain the ones that were already built. One problem was the shortage of missionaries, especially as the friars began to retire and leave. Fray Lasuén had asked the Catholic Church over and over to send replacements, but few new missionaries came.

Fray Lasuén died in 1803, before he had a chance to see things take a turn for the worse. In 1810, Spain had bigger problems and soon left the California missions to fend for themselves. The Mexican war for independence from Spain had begun, and back home, the Spanish were also at war with France. At the time, the friar in charge of Mission San Fernando Rey de España was Fray José Antonio Urrestí.

Spain no longer had a direct route to Alta California and could not afford to send supplies. Instead, the friars began trading with British and American trade ships to get the supplies they needed.

Soon, the Spanish government stopped paying wages to the soldiers. Instead of planting food to help themselves, the soldiers at nearby presidios put more pressure on the missions. They demanded food and other supplies from the missions, and as they became more ill-tempered, they treated the American Indians with cruelty. More and more neophytes fled the missions.

The neophyte community at Mission San Fernando was already shrinking from other causes. Many of the American Indians were dying from diseases, such as mumps, chickenpox, and the flu. These diseases, which were brought from Europe by the settlers, did not always kill the Europeans. However, they did kill many American Indians, whose bodies were not immune to them.

◀ *This painting depicts the war for Mexican independence.*

▲

Some mission Indians were mistreated by Spanish soldiers.

The community at Mission San Fernando had to struggle to supply the soldiers with food, clothing, and weapons. The friars were even forced to pay the soldiers' wages by giving them supplies from their annual stipends! Fray Ibarra, who took charge in 1820, wrote many letters to the commander of the troops complaining of the starvation that the neophytes suffered because of the soldiers' demands.

In addition to these problems, there was even less food. The harvests were not always large enough to feed so many people. Some of their crops were ruined by insects and wild animals. Caterpillars ate the bean crops, locusts destroyed the wheat fields, and rabbits and worms ruined the corn.

War Ends and Secularization Begins

In 1821, Mexico won independence from Spain. The new government of Mexico wanted more Mexicans to settle farms and towns in Alta California. However, most of the best lands belonged to the mission Indians and were being held in trust by the Church. The new Mexican officials decided to pass laws to secularize the missions. These laws would allow the Mexican government to take the control of the missions away from the Franciscan friars.

Under these new laws, the missions would be run by the Mexican government instead of the Church. The mission communities would become towns, and the mission churches would be led by priests who did not do missionary work. Then, all the neophytes would be free to leave the missions.

It was not until 1834 that Governor José Figueroa officially secularized Mission San Fernando. A plan was made to divide the land between settlers and neophytes. However, many settlers were greedy for the fertile farmlands, and the officials in charge of carrying out the plan for distribution of land were corrupt. Furthermore, the American Indians did not understand the concept of land ownership. For them, owning a piece of land was like owning a piece of sky or river!

Many of the American Indians did not want to be farmers. In the end, some American Indians went back to their mountain villages. Others went to work at ranches near the mission for little more than room and board. They were not treated much better than they had been at the mission, and often, they were treated worse. Many of the ex-neophytes never learned to be self-sufficient outside the mission.

Some Chumash Indians went back to their original villages.

The Mexican government's plan to reorganize Alta California included sending all Spanish-born friars back to Spain. Nevertheless, they allowed Fray Ibarra to stay at Mission San Fernando because they still needed someone to remain in charge. In 1835, however, Fray Ibarra decided to leave. He did not want to continue watching the decline of the mission.

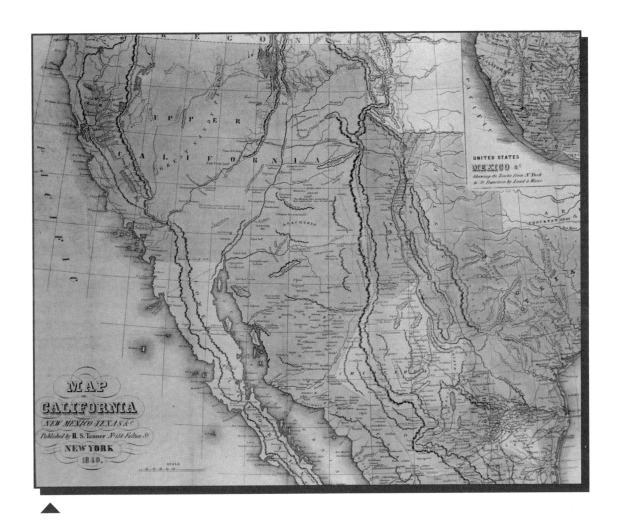

Alta California was renamed California in 1848.

Mexico's hold on California didn't last long. After a few years, the United States decided they wanted to own the land of Alta California. The Mexican War began and in 1848, Alta California became part of the United States. Alta California was then renamed California.

The Gold Rush

By the mid-1840s, more and more Americans were heading to California in wagon trains. One man, James Marshall, made a discovery that brought the world's attention to California: gold. Soon, not just Americans and American Indians were looking for gold in California, but Chinese, Latinos, Germans, Irish, French, and Turks. These foreigners worked the mines that were springing up everywhere.

The Gold Rush, as this period between 1849-1856 is called, spelled disaster for the American Indians of California. In truth, they had probably discovered the gold

The gold diggers that came to California were often cruel to the Indians.

centuries earlier, but had considered it no more valuable than turquoise or slate. Within a decade, as many as 100,000 of the 170,000 Indians living in California had died from violence, disease, and starvation. By 1900, the population of American Indians in California was below 16,000. The California Indians suffered greatly under Mexican and American occupation, more than they ever did under the Spanish mission system.

▲

Indians dying of sickness.

Legends of Mission San Fernando

The Reign of the Rats

Almost from the start, Mission San Fernando had a problem with rats. The rats ate everything that they could find. Once they found their way into the storerooms, the problem became serious. The missionaries at Mission San Gabriel had a solution. They sent a pair of cats to catch the rats at Mission San Fernando. This seemed to work until the friars realized that the cats could not go everywhere the rats did. To solve this, they cut holes in the corners of the thick mission doors big enough for the cats to walk through. This helped bring about the end of the rat problem.

Secret Gold

In March 1842, California gold was first discovered near Mission San Fernando. A story spread that the mission friars had known about the gold all along and had buried it in the mission grounds before they abandoned the missions. Treasure hunters came from the Los Angeles *pueblo* and other towns. They dug up the floors of the church at Mission San Fernando, but they never found hidden gold.

Gold Rush miners.

The mission was kept very clean, but was still overrun with rats. ▶

Nevertheless, the San Fernando Valley had hidden treasures elsewhere, and legend has it that $80,000 to $100,000 in gold dust was found in nearby rivers and stream beds.

The Fourth Bell

At Mission San Fernando, there were once four bells, which called the neophytes to meals, work, and prayer. Three of them hung in the bell tower and one of them hung at the west end of the *convento*. Around 1860, however, only three bells remained: one large bell and two smaller ones. What happened to the fourth bell?

The bell disappeared

The recovered fourth bell of Mission San Fernando.

until 1920, when it was found in an orange grove near the mission. It was identified as the missing bell from a cross and the letters *DE Sn FERNO* hammered onto its bronze surface. It had been removed and hidden in 1860 to save it from thieves.

Most of the mission bells came from Spain, Mexico, or Peru. Mission San Fernando's fourth bell was cast in 1796 in Alaska. A Russian count traded it for food in San Francisco, and from there it went to Mission San Fernando.

Myth of A Neophyte Artist

Many of the neophytes at Mission San Fernando were talented artisans. The same people who had painted designs on boulders and cave walls had turned their talents to the mission walls. Often, they combined American Indian and European images, which they copied from artwork brought from Europe. The most famous neophyte painter from Mission San Fernando was a man named Juan Antonio. He painted an important series of images of the death of Jesus Christ. In this artwork, the face of Jesus Christ has American Indian features.

Historians think there might be hidden meaning in Juan Antonio's painting. Some believe that the subject of the painting shows his Christian faith. Others believe the reason he painted the face of Jesus with American Indian features was to show that his people suffered the way Jesus did.

The Modern-Day Mission

Earthquakes damaged much of the mission.

Today, Mission San Fernando Rey de España can still be found in the city of Los Angeles. Over the years, it was severely damaged by earthquakes and vandalism. However, in 1974, the Roman Catholic Archdiocese of Los Angeles decided to build an exact replica of the original church. The last restoration effort, after another earthquake, was in 1996.

Because the mission is so close to Hollywood, it has been used for many movie location shootings. The mission is also a popular tourist destination. Visitors to the "long building" can see the huge winepress, smoke room, and refectory.

The *convento* now has one of the oldest libraries in California, containing books collected by the friars. This collection, which was once put in storage, had to be restored before being permanently

◀ The altar at Mission San Fernando.

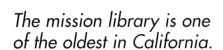

The mission library is one of the oldest in California.

▲
Living quarters of a friar.

▲
This statue of Mary stands in the church.

housed here. The gardens have also been brought back to their former glory. The original fountain still stands, but was moved 300 feet from its first location.

A beautiful park is now across the street from this historic landmark. At the entrance of the park is a statue of Fray Serra, with his arms around an American Indian boy. Fray Serra was given the honorific title "Blessed" by Pope John Paul II in September of 1988. Today, Fray Serra is a candidate for Catholic sainthood, an honor given to Catholics who have devoted their lives to good works.

Mission San Fernando today reminds us of the hopes and hard work of the friars and neophytes who made the mission an economic success. For some American Indians today, however, the missions are not monuments, but reminders of how people lost their

▲
This basket was made and used by the Chumash Indians.

native lands. For better or worse, the 21 Spanish Missions in California forever changed the lives of countless people.

At a park near the mission, stands this statue of Fray Serra and an Indian boy.

Make Your Own Model Mission

To make your own model of the San Fernando Rey de España mission, you will need:

foamcore

paint (cream, black, red, green)

lasagna

mini bells

cardboard

mini flowers/trees

floral foam blocks

tongue depressors

glue gun

glue sticks

pins

toothpicks

scissors

ruler

pencil

Directions:

Step 1: Use a piece of foamcore that is 20" x 20" for your mission base. Paint it cream color and let dry.

Adult supervision is suggested.

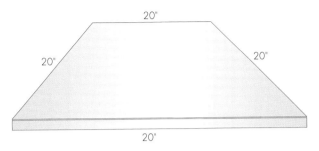

Step 2: Cut out 4 pieces of floral foam that are 3″ x 8″ and paint cream color. Let dry.

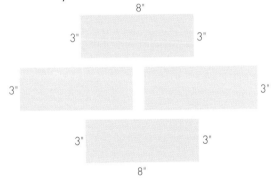

Step 3: Cut out 2 pieces from the floral foam that are 3″ x 3″ and 3″ x 5″. Paint cream color. Let dry.

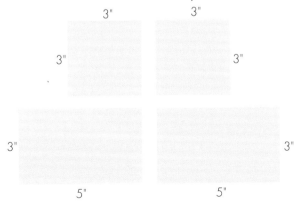

53

Step 4: Use pins to attach 4 floral foam blocks that are 3″ x 8″ to form a box shape. Place on mission base.

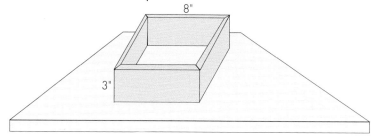

Step 5: Attach 2 pieces of floral foam that are 3″ x 3″ and 3″ x 5″ to the top of the mission front.

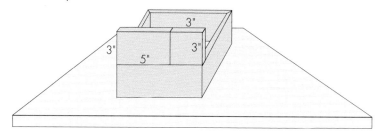

Step 6: Take lasagna pieces and break them through the wide part into 2 pieces that are 3″ long and 3 pieces that are 5″ long. Paint all pieces red and set aside.

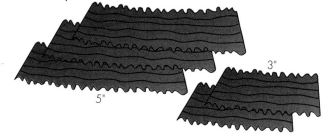

Step 7: Cut two 2 tongue depressors in half through the wide part and paint them black. Set aside.

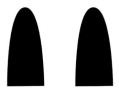

Step 8: To make roofs, cut out 2 cardboard pieces that are 2" x 6". Bend each in half. Pin one to each side of the church front.

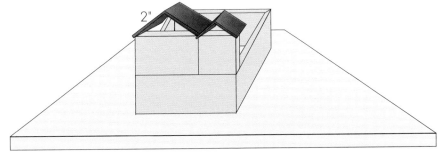

Step 9: Cut a piece of cardboard to measure 3" x 5". This will be for a terrace roof to the right and front of the church.

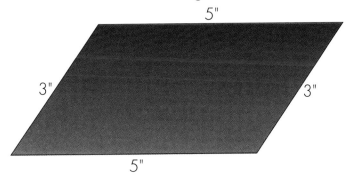

Step 10: To make the columns for the terrace roof, glue 3 glue gun sticks to the base on the right, front side of the church as shown.

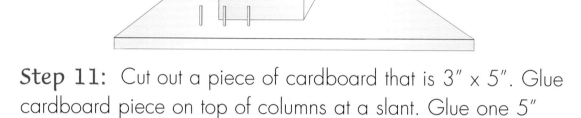

Step 11: Cut out a piece of cardboard that is 3" x 5". Glue cardboard piece on top of columns at a slant. Glue one 5" piece of lasagna on top of the terrace roof.

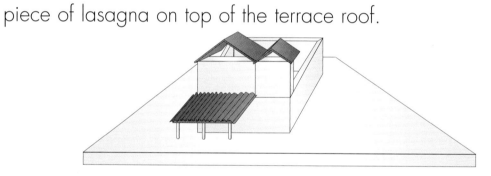

Step 12: Glue red lasagna pieces that are 3" long to the 3" church roofs. Glue the 2 pieces that are 5" long onto the 5" church roofs.

Step 13: Glue black tongue depressors onto the front of the church for windows. Glue one tongue depressor onto the left front side to make a doorway.

Step 14: Form a cross with toothpicks and attach to the top of the church building.

Step 15: Decorate with mini flowers and trees.

*Use the above mission as a reference for building your mission.

Important Dates in Mission History

1492	Christopher Columbus reaches the West Indies
1542	Cabrillo's expedition to California
1602	Sebastián Vizcaíno sails to California
1713	Fray Junípero Serra is born
1769	Founding of San Diego de Alcalá
1770	Founding of San Carlos Borromeo del Río Carmelo
1771	Founding of San Antonio de Padua and San Gabriel Arcángel
1772	Founding of San Luis Obispo de Tolosa
1775–76	Founding of San Juan Capistrano
1776	Founding of San Francisco de Asís
1776	Declaration of Independence is signed
1777	Founding of Santa Clara de Asís
1782	Founding of San Buenaventura
1784	Fray Serra dies
1786	Founding of Santa Bárbara
1787	Founding of La Purísima Concepción
1791	Founding of Santa Cruz and Nuestra Señora de la Soledad
1797	Founding of San José, San Juan Bautista, San Miguel Arcángel, and **San Fernando Rey de España**
1798	Founding of San Luis Rey de Francia
1804	Founding of Santa Inés
1817	Founding of San Rafael Arcángel
1823	Founding of San Francisco de Solano
1849	Gold found in northern California
1850	California becomes the 31st state

Glossary

baptism (BAP-tiz-um) A religious ceremony that represents washing away sins with water.

colonist (KOL-uh-nist) A person who settles in a new country.

convert (KON-vert) To cause someone to change a belief.

cremated (KREE-mayt-id) To reduce to ashes by burning.

expedition (EK-spe-dish-un) A journey taken for a special purpose.

fray (FRAY) The Spanish word for friar.

friar (FRY-ur) A brother in a communal religious order. Friars can also be priests.

Franciscan order (Fran-SIS-ken OR-dur) A part of the Catholic Church dedicated to preaching, missions, and charities.

granary (GRAH-na-ree) A windowless building used for storing grain.

mission (MISH-un) A church or religious center where missionaries work to help people in the community.

missionary (MIH-shun-ayr-ee) A person who teaches his or her religion to people with different beliefs.

neophyte (NEE-oh-fyt) A person who has recently converted to another religion.

quadrangle (KWAH-drang-ul) The square at the center of a mission that is surrounded by four buildings.

secularize (SEHK-yoo-luh-ryz) To make someone or something no longer religious.

self-sufficient (SELF-suh-FISH-ent) Able to provide for one's own needs without outside aid.

settlement (SEH-tul-ment) The act of occupying land and claiming it as one's own.

territory (TEHR-uh-tohr-ee) Land that is controlled by a person or a group of people.

Pronunciation Guide

atole (ah-tol-ay)

Chumash (CHOO-mahsh)

convento (kahn-VEN-toh)

El Camino Real (EL kah-MEE-noh RAY-al)

Kawenga (KAH-wen-gah)

monjerío (mohn-hayr-EE-oh)

Junípero Serra (YOO-ni-per-o SER-ra)

pueblos (PWAY-blohs)

San Fernando Rey de España (SAN fer-NAN-do rey day es-PAN-ya)

shinny (SHIN-ee)

siesta (see-EHS-tah)

tomol (TOH-mul)

Resources

To learn more about the California missions, check out these books and Web sites:

Books:
The California Missions by Elizabeth Van Steenwyk
Missions of the Los Angeles Area by Dianne McMillan
Missions of the Southern Coast by Nancy Lemoke

Web Sites:
http://tqd.advanced.org/3615/
http://home.earthlink.net/~foghorn1/
http://www.tsoft.net/~cmi/
http://www.ca-missions.org/

Index